LEARNING JOY

*A Book for Parents and Teachers
Who Want to Help Children
Find Themselves—and Joy*

by
Mimi Dickson
and
Jean Robitscher

WHITMORE PUBLISHING COMPANY
Ardmore, Pennsylvania

To my children and grandchildren, who have given me a sense of joy.

Mimi Dickson

To my daughter, Jan, one of Mimi's special children.

Jean Begeman Robitscher

Contents

Acknowledgments

For his loving attitude, liberating me to do what I love best, my thanks go to my husband, Pem.

For their love and understanding in helping me teach joy, my thanks go to Adeline Edwards and Betty McCorkel.

For the opportunity and freedom to teach my own way, my thanks go to the Swarthmore Presbyterian Church and the members of the board, auxiliary, and staff of the Child Guidance and Mental Health Clinics of Delaware County.

For making the facilities of the clinic available to the children through endless hours of driving, my thanks go to the Wheels for Welfare volunteers.

For their encouragement and interest, my thanks go to Ruth Malone; Virginia Dudley; Yvonne McCabe; Lilah Thayer; my devoted son-in-law, Henry McCorkle; and Eleanor Langdon, who transcribed countless tapes.

For giving me professional support during my unconventional career, my thanks go to Dr. Jonas Robitscher and the late Dr. Frederick Dudley.

For transmitting my thoughts and experiences in such a skillful way that I might help others through this book, my thanks go to Jean Robitscher.

Mimi
(Helen Porter Dickson)

Foreword

Mimi Dickson is a calm and determined woman who sees life as an opportunity to fulfill the needs of others. She has used her abilities to pioneer in early childhood development, and her interest later broadened to include equally pioneering work in the therapy of autistic children.

What is remarkable is that Mimi made her contributions in these fields without formal training. Or perhaps it is not remarkable—a degree in education might have turned Mimi into a conventional pedagogue instead of the warm, mothering person she is. It might have set up barriers of traditional methods and bureaucratic procedures that would have kept Mimi separate from "her" children.

We first met Mimi through our own unmet need—our daughter had been born with congenital cataracts; and although three "needling" operations had restored some vision to her, she still operated somewhat as a blind child would. We had moved to a new community, Swarthmore, Pennsylvania, and lived in an older neighborhood, where Jan had virtually no playmates. At the age of three, she was totally dependent upon parental presence for security. We knew she needed other relationships. Mimi accepted her in her nursery school. She *wanted* Jan because, as she explained to us then, she felt that her nursery school would not only serve this "special" child, but having such children in the school would be helpful to the "normal" children, who would learn to get pleasure in helping others and also would learn that there is much imperfection in our world. She would include several "different" children—their special quality might relate to physical, psychological, or ethnic differences. Jan flourished, making her first strides toward independence and self-sufficiency. Her life might have been quite different without such early experience.[1]

Through the years, we followed Mimi's work and wondered at her results. She had opened her nursery school, although she was an unaccredited teacher, in 1950 at the Swarthmore Presbyterian Church. The minister there recognized her intuitive understanding of the needs of children, and her school became an integral part of the community. It provided a workshop in child care for Swarthmore College and Swarthmore High School students. In the early 1950s, long before school integration was the norm, Mimi encouraged black parents in the community to send their children to her school. At one time she had three black staff members—and that was unusual, too, then: a music teacher, a shop carpenter, and an assistant teacher. Mimi headed the school for ten years and trained the staff that succeeded her.

Later, at a time when most other people are glad to be retired, Mimi expanded her interests to include the needs of severely psychologically damaged children under the auspices of the Delaware County Child Guidance Clinic. Our mutual friend, Dr. Frederick Dudley, a child psychiatrist and head of the Clinic, and I were enthusiastic about making use of her talents in spite of the lack of conventional qualifications.

This would not be considered unusual today. We are now in a period when indigenous mental health workers and "street people" are accepted as part of the helping professions. But when Dr. Dudley hired Mimi to undertake the task of structuring a day-care program to help autistic children, it was considered a courageous step on both their parts.

Many student teachers have worked with Mimi, and there have been many attempts to get her to put down on paper her way of relating to children, which combines warmth and discipline. Much of what Mimi does is instinctual, and finding the words in order to pass on her experience has been difficult. Over the years my wife, Jean², has tried to push Mimi into writing this book, tape recording Mimi's expressions and philosophy and some of her experiences with specific children to use as a foundation.

In the final analysis, Jean and I found that much of what happens in the interaction between Mimi and "her" children cannot be put on paper. It is ironic that much of what is taught in programs of education does not produce good teachers, and many of the qualities of a good teacher cannot be formally learned.

The essence of Mimi is her interest in and identification with the child with whom she is working; and much of what is included in the process of "professionalization" in degree programs is merely learning to put protective barriers between the teacher and her charges.

Mimi's philosophy in seeing her children return to the real world healthier and happier is contained in this adage: "What you give away you keep, and what you keep you lose." Many of Mimi's ideas respecting the dignity of children, not allowing permissiveness to deteriorate into complete lack of structure, working with parents and family along with the child to emphasize the diadic relationship of child and adult, sound less revolutionary now than they did three decades ago when she began. If we had succeeded in getting Mimi to write her book earlier, she might have gained more credit as a pioneer. But we are sure that Mimi is not interested in credit. She will feel her book is useful if some of her hard-learned experience can be recycled through a parent and teacher to fulfill their needs and the needs of a child.

We have always felt that Mimi has the same spirit that caused Sylvia Ashton-Warner to write in *Teacher:*

> I don't even claim to be a teacher at all. I'm just a nitwit somehow let loose among children. If only I kept workbooks and made schemes and taught like other teachers I should have the confidence of numbers. It's the payment, the price of walking alone. . . . I've got to do what I believe. And I

believe in all I do. It's this price one continually pays for stepping out of line. I'm feeling too old to pay it. But I _must_ do what I believe in or nothing at all. Life's so short.

Jonas Robitscher, M.D., J.D.[3]
February 1977

---

1. Jan Robitscher graduated from DePauw University in 1976 and is now in graduate school at Notre Dame University.
2. Jean Begeman Robitscher, editor, author, and free-lance writer, encouraged Mimi to record her teaching methods and philosophy. Using the tapes, along with personal interview sessions and common recollections, Jean and Mimi produced this book with the hope that teachers and parents might find it helpful.
3. Dr. Robitscher, who encouraged Mimi to pursue her unique work with autistic children, practiced psychiatry and psychoanalysis and taught forensic psychiatry at Villanova University and the University of Pennsylvania for many years before moving to Atlanta, Georgia, where he is the first occupant of the Henry R. Luce Chair of Law and the Behavioral Sciences at Emory University.

I

Born to Teach

Every child has a right to be a happy, whole, free individual. To accomplish this, the child must learn to measure unconsciously his or her own capabilities. I am speaking of the normal child as well as the "special" child, one who is emotionally or physically damaged.

Teachers have always been an important part of my life. I was a professor's daughter on a New England campus, exposed early and often to my parents' faculty friends. During my high school years in Worcester, Massachusetts, I had a remarkable teacher, Margarette Knight. She looked like Beatrix Potter, the beloved creator of *Peter Rabbit*. As a teacher, she was no less talented. Robert Benchley was one of her protégés, and I credit her with sending him forth to give my generation style and wit. She also befriended me.

I feel now that she gave me direction and self-confidence, enabling me to help hundreds of children find joy and creativity, which are the warp and the woof of a finely patterned fabric. I knew even then that, like Miss Knight, I would be a teacher.

My father, James P. Porter, was dean of men and head of the psychology department at Clark University, which was the seat of the newborn science of psychology at the time. He was also a naturalist and would spend hours showing me the intricate designs of spider webs or finding an ant hill to explain to me how ant colonies work. We had beehives outside the kitchen window. Everything was a learning experience.

My father's friends, including the eminent Ernest Jones, biographer of Sigmund Freud, would visit and I would listen, always learning. Books were everywhere. I loved to hold them even before I could read.

Later on, my father moved the family to Athens, Ohio, where he was editor of the *Journal of Applied Psychology* and head of the psychology department at Ohio University. I believe I absorbed some psychology by osmosis during this period.

I attended Swarthmore College to major in history. There I met and married Pemberton Dickson, stopped school to be a homemaker (which was the fashion in those days), and gave priority to being the mother of our three daughters. Still, even without credentials, I knew I would someday teach.

My first opportunity came during World War II. I took charge of a group of preschool children at Friends Central School in Philadelphia and later directed a summer camp program at the progressive Rose Valley School. My theories on child care and training were crystallizing with each experience. I decided to have my own school, one which would not be a child care center but would help each child develop his abilities to capacity.

The idea did not seem so complicated. I did not feel hampered by my lack of a degree of formal training in the field of child development. As I explored the possibility of starting a preschool nursery, I felt that one needed only the kind of experience I had as a mother and one who loves children.

My philosophy then, as now, was simply: Every child has a right to be a happy, whole, free individual. To accomplish this, the child must learn to unconsciously measure his or her own capabilities. I am speaking of the normal child as well as the "special" child who is emotionally or physically damaged.

It has been a great many years since I began working professionally with children. During the first phase of my teaching, I dealt primarily with normal pre-school and kindergarten children; later with children who had severe emotional components, often diagnosed as autistic or unable to communicate.

For the most part, I treated both the same. I have always felt that teaching children of whatever mental or physical capacity requires the same approach. In both, there is challenge and demand. In both, I suppose, you might say I have adhered to the Bruno Bettleheim stricture: "Love is not enough." Children need, from their teachers as well as their parents, to be treated with dignity.

Children are born with an ability to love. They are born with dignity. I have seen them stripped of both before they were old enough to enter nursery school. They are the ones for whom, then, we must add *learning joy* to their curriculum.

In 1950, with the encouragement of Dr. Joseph Bishop, who was then pastor of the Swarthmore Presbyterian Church, I opened the nursery school to children of all races and religions. Of course, this concept is law today, but at that time it was unique.

When the black children of the Swarthmore community could not afford the school, I would arrange a scholarship so they would be able to attend. I hired three remarkable black teachers, Mrs. Adeline Edwards, who was in charge of the music hour; a shop carpenter, John Pierce; and Mrs. Helen Johnson. The staff included, over the years, Margaret Price, a veteran of the Swarthmore public school system, and Ruth Webb, a young psychologist, who was confined to an electric wheelchair because of a severe muscular impediment from cerebral palsy. She would observe the children and write reports to the parents, and her quiet observations and intuitive nature made her a valuable addition to the staff. At another time, I hired the wife of a couple

from India who had moved to Swarthmore. She brought to the children a sense of beauty with her colorful saris and graceful manners. Betty McCorkel, who has steadfastly supported all of my ideas and teaching principles, is now head of the school, giving continuity and dedication to another generation.

Along with children of all races, we accepted children with physical or emotional differences. Each year we would have several who were polio victims (in the pre-Salk-vaccine days), others who were handicapped in various ways, deaf, or with serious eye defects. I have always felt that normal children benefit from the presence of these special children. Sometimes they would hardly notice that a playmate was in any way different. If they noticed and made a remark, we would say, "He is learning." And very often the children *would* learn, making tremendous strides toward independence and self-sufficiency. Their parents, who unconsciously may have been holding back the child, would be gratified and amazed at the results.

I have always stressed *respect*. Children need to be accepted and loved the way they are as individuals, not just as an extension of the parent. Early in my teaching career, I banished the terms *good* and *bad*. If a child's behavior seemed undesirable, the child, I would point out, needed to learn better behavior. One who was learning did not need to feel guilty or unworthy—there was no stigma to the word, because we were all learning something at all times.

Only by respecting the children ourselves can we expect them to learn to respect others. To help a child respect himself is to help him care for his own needs, express his ideas and feelings, control his emotions, and know how to relate to others.

Children know when they are not measuring up to a situation, and that is why it is so important to help them become pleased with themselves. Our school would help the child develop his emotional and physical stability by fulfilling his own potentialities in every phase of school activity.

I would often say, "Mimi is proud of you," when the student showed me a picture or reached a new stage of development or control. One time I received a card from a high school student who was one of my preschoolers. He wrote, "Mimi, I still do things now because I know that you know I can do them."

Along with the word *respect*, I would like to add another word to the fabric we will weave in this attempt to create a pattern for our children. The word is *expectation*. From the beginning, a child can sense the expectation of the adults around him. He responds eagerly and happily to both respect and expectation. Reasonable standards of behavior, reasonable demands for growth and self-discipline, can provide a welcome spur for him.

A little boy came into the nursery school one day, accompanied by a fearful mother and a rather austere father. The child was covered with eczema, and he scratched incessantly, nervously. We noted that when he became absorbed in something outside himself, playing games or singing songs during the music period, he did not have the time to scratch. We would mention this to him and talk to him about it.

When I bade him good-bye for the weekend, after his second week in the school, I took him by the hand and said, "Now, remember, Mimi wants you to go slow. When you feel yourself getting ready to scratch, you just begin thinking about something else! Say to yourself, 'Mimi is trying to help me not to scratch.'"

When he came back on Monday he was all smiles. "I tried hard, Mimi."

"Well!" I said, "I can *see* you have!" His skin was not angry red, the way it usually was, and the hair on the top of his head was shiny and clean. He moved more slowly and seemed less nervous. All of this in only two weeks time, all because he wanted to fulfill my expectations.

Children know far more than most adults realize about what is really going on within the family structure. Honesty is a part of the child's natural equipment; he knows when he is being lied to, when someone is being condescending, and when he is being shortchanged.

He is being shortchanged whenever he is not required to live up to his capacity. The vision a good parent will hold before his child is always that he is being expected to meet certain standards, that he is expected to behave like a three-year-old, four-year-old, or six-year-old, whichever he is. As a corollary, the parent will as a matter of course help him in every way to achieve his capacity. This is just as true for the "normal"child as for the handicapped or emotionally disturbed child.

I often wonder if the parents of these children ever ask themselves, "How do I let my child's handicap influence the way I plan his daily routine?" Working every day with them, as I have, I find it significant as a standard that they be held to capacity at all times, not given in to because of the adult's feelings of guilt or responsibility or pity. More important than any other factor for their future growth is the discipline and loving firmness of the adults in their lives.

Too often today, I believe, the troubles of young people can be traced back to the question of what the adults in their lives actually expected of them. Many seem to have no goals, no incentives, no standards to achieve. Too many have too much done for them. Too many luxuries, near at hand, are substituted for the genuinely loving demand that the child grow and mature.

Along with our great expectations, there must be some restrictions. At the school we imposed limits of normal behavior within the group and we would ask the parents to do the same at home. As the child grows and learns, I am reminded of putting an amaryllis in a pot. The amaryllis will not bloom unless it is held firmly in closed quarters. We must hold our children firmly in our hearts and in our arms. Then when we let them go free, they bloom, just like the amaryllis.

II

A Pattern of Rhythm

At the end of my life when I felt I should have been getting ready to retire, two of the doctors at the Child Guidance Clinic of Delaware County* who were longtime friends of mine approached me about a new project. Dr. Fred Dudley and Dr. Jonas Robitscher both thought my temperament and experience, if not my academic credentials, made me suited to head the clinic's day school for emotionally disturbed and autistic children.

I did not know the meaning of the word *autistic* then. Not many other people did either. The more we discussed my role, the more I realized that this new challenge would be the one for which I had truly prepared myself. All of my ideas about handling children with dignity and respect, holding out expectations, giving them love, could be used to the fullest. All of my experience as a nursery school teacher dealing with parents, encouraging them to change their attitudes, and listening to their frustrations and hopes would be utilized. And so, although I was approaching sixty, I started another phase of my life as a teacher.

The clinic was located in Media, only a few miles from Swarthmore. I felt I could not go without Adeline, who had brought music to all of my children and with whom I had developed a

---

*The official title of the clinic today is Child Guidance and Mental Health Clinics of Delaware County, Media, Pennsylvania.

very special relationship. Her responses to the children were intuitively correct. Her joyful manner somehow gave me the courage to tackle any situation. She agreed to come along.

My approach to children was so simple I wondered briefly whether I would have to change my approach for these highly disturbed and uncommunicative children. I thought not. I would handle them just as I handled the most normal of the Swarthmore nursery school group.

It is just as important for the autistic child as it is the normal one to find his capacity, to hold to a pattern that he himself can control. I have always called it a "pattern of rhythm." We help the child to slowly move ahead, and then let go. We would work with a child steadily for two or three days, and then we would step back and watch the child move alone. This pattern of rhythm, like the waves on a beach washing back and forth, seems to work. We give the child understanding, patience, tremendous belief in him, and respect, and then we watch him hold it and carry it with him.

I was inspired by the message the Child Guidance Clinic gave in its brochure for those interested in the work that was being done there:

> Every child needs his own island . . . his own special identity. He must also have life lines strong and sure to other larger islands—his home and parents, his school, his friends.
> If his island is uncertain and shaky and the lines thin and unpredictable, this child feels lost and insecure. He is afraid to relate to others—he is afraid to reach out. This is what we mean by emotional disturbance.
> Helping a child to establish an island of his own from which he can reach out is a job for many.
> The Child Guidance Clinic staff of psychiatrists, psychologists and social workers form a "team" working with and through the parents and the child. They help the disturbed child to secure firmer footing on his island and to strengthen the life lines on which he must depend to grow into a healthy adult.

As the children were brought to me and as the conferences with their parents and foster parents and caseworkers began, I learned about autism. These children seemed to have special traits—some wanted only to be alone; others did not seem to mind company but were obsessive about certain things, such as what they ate or a certain object or toy. Often sound or noise would cause them to be anxious. Some were fearful, bland, distrusting. Others revealed traits of brilliance or at least a phenomenal memory, even though they spoke not a word. Another would suddenly show humor with a wink at an appropriate time. It was all a mystery to me; and so I would learn with them, I decided, from the beginning of my new teaching career at the clinic.

There are few clues to the cause of autism. Sometimes the

children do not appear sick or even abnormal. The doctors frequently find no obvious brain damage, prenatal or natal, no pathology or inborn chemical errors of metabolism. There seem to be no genetic or hereditary disorders. Often the family of one autistic child has one or more normal children.

It became apparent to me that the children belonged in a day-care clinic, not in some isolated home situation or a cold institutional setting. They needed stimulation and guidance. They needed direction and affection. My staff and I were there to provide it.

It was not long before I had set the routine of our sessions with the children within the setting of the clinic. The doors were never locked; the weather would never prevent us from taking a long walk and exploring nature; the activities geared to each child individually gave each a chance to grow and learn in a setting filled with hope and joy rather than frustration and hostility.

In our nursery unit at the Delaware County Child Guidance Clinic, we would see a new child on the first day for a half hour (with his mother and father, if possible, present) and the second day for three quarters of an hour and the third day a two-hour period. He would then join either the morning or the afternoon nursery unit. Each child received individual psychotherapy, and the parents or foster parents were counseled by a social worker. Only a few of the children in the beginning were diagnosed as autistic. Most of the others had severe behavior problems that kept them from being able to function in a normal school environment. Often the parents could not cope with them at home. They were children whose rhythm of life had been disturbed— sometimes because family crisis had separated them from their parents or because their mothers, for some reason, were not available to meet their emotional needs. Because of the home situations, they were confused and bewildered.

There had been so much harshness in their lives that in some ways they seemed older and more sophisticated than many youngsters. We tended to think of them as "little people" rather than children. It was our job to restore structure to their lives and draw them back into the mainstream of life.

The nursery unit provided for the most part the only stability in the children's daily lives. I am sure the clinic today continues somewhat along the lines of my routine. But I felt the importance of structure in the lives of these special children; so I planned the routine in this way. During the first two weeks, the child was allowed to wander and observe and find his way. We would discover how much adult direction he could take, and we began to treat him as a normal, whole child. This was a slow process and had to be done with a great deal of respect and love.

The program consisted of, first, a half-hour "work period." The children were exposed to all types of activities. Each was given the freedom to wander, to feel, to touch, to look, and to listen. And then the adult would move in slowly and help him put the boards and the boxes out or climb the ladders and guide his play toward a goal.

This was followed by the "toilet period." Again, this was done with respect and gentleness. If the child was not yet toilet trained, we would go through this very slowly and always with expectation that soon he would be in control of the situation. It was often not long before the child would feel this warmth and respect and respond.

There followed a "rest period," and the child would put down his mat to rest. It might take a long time and much firmness and help from the adult to make this a happy experience for the child. But again, the child would soon learn to enjoy this period, listening to records or a story, or just sitting by an adult so that if the child needed to touch the adult's hand or knee, he would know someone was there. The child would soon learn to fold his mat neatly and would be proud of this accomplishment.

After resting, there was the "lunch period." This, too, would become a happy, growing experience. We would have conversations at the lunch table, the subjects varying from food favorites to what it was to tell a "real" story and what it was to

tell a "pretend" story. We would try to make it a pleasant occasion.

Sometimes, of course, milk was spilled or one child would refuse to sit still; but after repetition and help from the adult, the child would learn. Soon they would take pride in going to get the wastebasket, setting out the milk cups, putting the chairs back in place.

Lunch would be followed by a "music period." Although we would get very little response at first, it was amazing to watch a child learn to listen, think, and relax. We liked to play folk songs like Burl Ives's "Blue Tail Fly" and more sophisticated music rather than the simple nursery rhymes. We used songs that challenged their imaginations. When they responded, in some amazing way they knew they had achieved something for their very own—adding a valuable piece to the structure they were beginning to build, an image of self. Several of the autistic children first began to sing the words of songs before they began to talk in sentences.

The nervous tensions of these disturbed children can be decreased by physical activity. We stressed heavy boards and heavy boxes, ladders to climb and barrels to push. We would teach them to roll on the grass or the floor and turn somersaults. I believe that by using their arms and legs in a rhythm of activity they use their energy in a productive way and are better able to relax. We would take long walks for exercise and to help the children see the beauty of plants and trees. They learned to walk, to control their desire to run away or to dart about. When we walked together, we would hold hands, and we would feel there was a relationship which was dignified and warm and very necessary to the growth of the child.

During our morning hour of strenuous activity, we noticed that the children would begin to hum and make noises. Later they would say words and often sentences. As they discovered their arms and legs and hands and worked with them in a constructive way, they became more relaxed and satisfied with themselves. They had more respect for their persons. As soon as we could help them participate as much as possible in the way that normal children would, I knew they had gained more self-respect. When they continued to progress, I knew they had found a "pattern of rhythm."

III
Parent Problems and Solutions

The word *parent* does not mean "pal." I do not care for the "pal" approach to parenthood. But I do feel that a parent should be a friend. A friend is an understanding person, and that is what we need in a parent—a person who is ready to reassure you when doubts or fears or unhappiness try to overtake you.

It is often reassuring to a child or a young person who is burdened with a problem to have his parents offer to talk about it and help him decide how to help himself. It is more important to reach down and help a child up than to talk down to him. It is better to be a friend than to be a disciplinarian.

When I was first married and had my first child, I felt a tremendous joy and thankfulness that I had a small baby to hold and to love and to guide. Then the neighbors and my mother-in-law would tell me not to do this or be careful about that. I became filled with fears. With the next child and the next, I realized how unfounded my fears were; and so I know it is important to help other parents learn to enjoy their children and help children learn the joy of living.

I have a favorite motto: "What you give away you keep, and what you keep you lose." There are variations of this idea. I understand one is an old German quotation: "What I spent I had; what I saved I lost; what I gave I have."

The common thread is obvious. By sharing ourselves with our children, our family, and our friends, we stand to gain. If we do not, we lose.

Our children do not belong to us just because we have given birth or provided a home. They are ours to guide, love, and protect only as long as they need us.

Dr. Benjamin Spock once wrote: "A satisfactory identification (with parents) depends on the adult's warmth, approval and capacity to share pleasures. A child especially needs support during periods of regression and loss of control. It is by learning that there are many people who can given him affection and support that a child is prepared to become an adult who cares about many people."

Dr. William R. Crawford, child psychoanalyst at the Institute of the Pennsylvania Hospital before his untimely death in his early forties, due to a heart attack, addressed a group of parents at a private school located on the affluent Main Line. He spelled out clearly the series of progression and regression that children go through in various stages of development that lead toward health and normality and eventually emotional maturity. Here are his criteria for *emotional maturity:*

1. Emotional independence and a reasonable dependence
2. Increased productive activity
3. Freedom from inferiority feelings, egotism, and competitiveness
4. Mature sexual attitudes
5. Control of hostilities; a reasonable aggressiveness
6. A firm sense of reality
7. Flexibility and adaptability
8. Capacity to love someone else, but with an enlightened self-interest

He believed that there were two important practical stages in the development of the conscience of the child.

The first stage is during early childhood, *ages one to seven,* when the basic underlayer is formed; when *the parent has the opportunity—as never again in the child's life—to establish a self-regulating apparatus in the child via prohibitions and restrictions;* when their willingness to love includes a willingness to punish; when limits are clearly, firmly, and consistently set; and when children have seen that the outside world is a force to be reckoned with, and at the same time realize the thrill of impulse control and self-mastery.

The second stage occurs when a child is about ten or twelve, when parents and parent-surrogate figures should shift from limit setting to example setting, combined with a willingness to allow children in these early years to learn by experience. Parents, teachers, and relatives become models, and though the child does not usually imitate them outright, he unconsciously adopts characteristics here and there from many. Most essential at this time is a shift of gears for parents. They should continue to define clearly their views on ethical, religious, and political matters but *not* insist on conformity with these views. The adolescent needs to know where his elders stand, and they should clarify their character for his benefit, but then they should allow him unconsciously to pick and choose the various character elements he is to absorb into his own personality.

Dr. Crawford's message includes a warning to the parents that "overgratification or overdeprivation in any of the stages of development can lead to regression or fixation at those stages of infantility." This we all know now. The busy life of so many parents who may give *things* and immediate gratification to their children instead of themselves is ever present, subtle though it may be.

Interviewing parents through the years has revealed to me that many young people who get married do not understand the responsibilities that go with it. They do not realize that a marriage is the beginning of something and not the end, that it demands a great deal of giving, that it demands most of all respect for themselves. More than once I have turned to a parent and said, "Don't be so hard on yourself. Love yourself a little more. Be proud of yourself. You're a child of God."

I have been heartened by the increasing recognition in recent years that children are individuals even when they are very young and that early childhood experiences will leave their mark. This is something that mothers recognized naturally during a time when mothering skills were absorbed as if by osmosis and passed along from generation to generation.

With the decline of the old-fashioned family, parents find themselves without models, and many parents I have seen think of their young children as either inanimate objects or intriguing toys in their earliest stages of development. Now psychologists tell us what some of us did not need to be told: that an infant even before he learns language is an active participant in his or her world, and the relationship between an infant and those who take care of him or her is an enormously rich and complicated interaction. I have been very happy to read about the methods of Dr. Frederick Leboyer, the French obstetrician, who wants every child to be born peacefully in a darkened, quiet environment. Dr. Leboyer fosters the interaction of mother and child immediately after birth. I am not in a position to judge the scientific validity of the results which seem to show that mother and child relate better to each other when "birth without violence" is practiced, but symbolically this seems a way of reestablishing natural patterns of parent-child relating with which civilization and "scientific medicine" have interfered.

I am always glad when I hear of any movement to foster good early mother-child and father-child relationships—hospital rooming-in so infants are not kept in impersonal nurseries, breast feeding so infants can enjoy the warmth and tactile stimulation as well as the nourishment that they derive from their mothers; straps and slings that enable young mothers and fathers to keep their children close by them, not propped up in stiff plastic carriers or left behind with baby-sitters.

When I was head of the nursery school at the Swarthmore Presbyterian Church, I jotted down questions parents should ask themselves once in a while to remind them of some of the simple principles of parenthood. I found later that these questions were just as applicable to the parents of our disturbed children in the Child Guidance Clinic. The list would change and grow longer:

1. If I were now my child's age, would I enjoy living with the kind of parent that I think I am?
2. Do I allow upsetting circumstances not related to my child to make me cross and unreasonably irritable with him? Am I honest about my moods and feelings about the child?
3. Am I a happy parent? Do I enjoy being with my child and talking to him?
4. Do I welcome and encourage my child to share his experiences with me?
5. Do I usually give my child a happy "Good morning"?
6. Is my discipline of my child consistent and logically based on fundamental rules of conduct which he accepts? Are my words consistent with my actions?
7. Do I allow unrealistic fears or guilt about my child to influence my planning of his daily program and future needs?
8. Do I trust my child?
9. Do I think of my child as a growing person and a future adult?
10. Do I confide in the child as a recognized member of the family?
11. Are my expectations of my child's performance (such as in eating, sleeping, playing) based upon his real capacity?
12. Am I alert to my child's needs? Do I know when he needs to talk and when he needs to be left alone? Am I available for regular or on-the-spot heart-to-heart talks?
13. Am I relaxed and happy at mealtime? How much does an untouched or picked-at meal disturb me? Am I honest with my child about these feelings? Do I feed him according to his needs?
14. Am I able to laugh with my child at my own mistakes? Do I accept his mistakes as learning opportunities for him?
15. Do I remember to fulfill my own needs for rest, recreation, and education?
16. Do I permit my child to impose upon me and to interfere

with my responsibilities to myself and my community?

17. Do I try to see the world as it looks to my child? Do I get down on the floor to play with him at regular times?

18. Do I encourage the growth of our child's imagination and his wonder of the world around him by sharing walks, excursions to buildings, projects, zoos with him? Do I share his joy of exploration?

19. Do I have, or am I building, a secure philosophy of life which is transmitted to my child more by attitude, ease, and warmth than by words?

I would like to see our young parents take a greater interest in creating a home. Homemaking is becoming one of the lost arts of America. I have noticed today that many busy parents, especially families with professional fathers who often work late, have the habit of feeding the children early and then having what they describe as "a peaceful dinner" later. Well, they have lost the joy of eating together as a family; they are depriving their children of this growth experience. There is joy in sitting around a table talking, exchanging ideas, listening to each other. This feeling of being together is transferred to the children, who pick up and form their own thoughts and beliefs. Perhaps if more families did this there would not be such a need for young people to join odd religious sects or isolated "cultist" communities, because the tremendous power of the home can extend outward as well as inward.

I am happy so many young people today are learning to bake bread. It was almost a lost art. We taught it at the nursery. We would bake muffins or bread and then eat it around the table together.

When Sarla Agarwal from India helped me teach, she would show the children how to make the flat pancakes that are like bread in India. People laugh when I say I think there would be fewer divorces in the world if there were more bread being baked in the kitchen! I know better, but I rationalize the statement by

saying, "Who could leave a house that smells like home-baked bread?" We need to return to the basics.

It is important for families to go out to dinner occasionally so that children learn how to behave in a restaurant, to lower their voices and not feel hurried when waiting to be served. The way you speak to the person waiting on you helps a child learn courtesy and thoughtfulness.

I am still learning as a grandmother as well as a teacher, and I like to share my experiences with the parents who come to me for advice. I have the compassion and eagerness to share with them the simplicity of what it takes to love and to enjoy our children, to be firm with them, to have expectations for them, to guide them, to demand their best, to be sure that they are ready when they are asking us to help them grow, to be not too busy to listen when they want to talk to us, to be available at all times until they are ready to walk alone. It is all so simple that I am almost embarrassed when anybody asks me to discuss it.

A recent visit with my daughter and grandchildren provided an experience of learning worth recording. It was a cool morning in May in New England, and we were on the last day of a delightful visit together. My youngest grandchild slipped off his chair and ran out to get his tricycle and rode off to the top of the drive on the hill. As he went out I said to my daughter, "Don't you feel that he needs a jacket?" She said, "No, he'll come in if he's cold and put it on." I have heard this remark from other young mothers, and I guess I started thinking about it. I went to the hall closet and picked up his little red baseball jacket that he liked very much and matching red baseball cap, and I went out to the top of the hill in the driveway and stood by the lamppost.

We are very fond of one another, and he seemed glad to see me. He came up quite close and circled around me. Then he came again, looked up at me, and said, "I don't need my jacket. I'm not cold."

But then he came around again, close to me. I put my hand down and I took hold of the handlebars of the tricycle. Then I took his little hand and I slipped on a sleeve. I put it around his shoulders, and he slipped his own hand in the other sleeve. Then I put his little cap on the top of his head with the visor in back, which is the way he liked it, and patted it. He looked up and smiled, and I said, "Whenever you get warm enough, you may take it off." Then I walked back into the house.

I feel quite strongly that this is the way we should help all people, especially little children, to start the day. Maybe I should broaden that and say to start their lives—and we have to repeat it many, many times. We have to reach out our hands and start them off and let them decide when they are ready to walk alone. When we give just a little pat, an encouraging smile, or a wink, it is often enough to start them off on the right foot.

That evening, as I left to go home, my son-in-law drove me to the airport. He began discussing a friend of theirs whose daughter was in college and most unhappy. The daughter held this unhappiness within her until this year. She was going to be a senior. She finally had the courage to write to her mother and tell her that she had never had a date at college and had just about had enough of feeling inferior and sad.

The mother and father are very social people, popular and outgoing and attractive, busy with their own lives. The mother talks a lot of her own childhood, and one has an uncomfortable feeling that she is enjoying her memories more than her motherhood.

Again I felt that here was a mother not giving her daughter, who is lovely and has a good mind to share with other people, the pat she needed. The mother seemed unaware of the tremendous capabilities she had. She should have forgotten herself and extended her warmth and understanding to her child. It is never too late. If she could give her a feeling of pride in herself, it would be as warm and helpful as a little red jacket.

In our nursery school unit, I have to tell the parents often to watch for similar signs of growing pains. I tell them that a three-year-old must be a three-year-old for a whole year, a four-year-old must be a four-year-old for a whole year, and a five-year-old must be a five-year-old for a whole year. There may be days when they act ten and there may be days when they act two, but it is our own respect and ability to observe and not to interfere except for guidance and a little push now and then that lets them grow. We have to know when to move back and let them take over.

One time, when I was working at the clinic, a young mother asked me if she could take her son to see *Mary Poppins*. Tommy was one of our most disturbed autistic children, a very brilliant boy, confused and unhappy. They had given him everything he wanted but without understanding. He was walking to the car with us when she asked about the movie. Tommy knew exactly what we were discussing. I looked at him, and he returned a knowing glance. So I said, "Perhaps you had better ask Tommy if he's ready."

We parents need to ask: Are they ready? Are we asking too much of them too soon? Are we giving them too little when they need more? Are our expectations deep enough that they feel respect and our belief in them as individuals with frailties just like ours? If they understand this, I think that they will learn to walk alone and learn to ask for help when they need it and learn to give it to others as well as to themselves.

In this book there is a purpose in my not always stating whether I am talking about an autistic child or one who entered the clinic as emotionally disturbed. They need the same kind of attention and love. So do normal children. So do the children who are retarded or brain-damaged through some terrible accident.

There was a mother in Walnut Creek, California, whose three-year-old daughter proved the miracle of mothering, in my opinion. The child had been found floating facedown in the family pool. The doctors at the hospital where she had been taken told her that because of a lack of oxygen the child's brain was ruined. "Think of her as dead," they said, incredible as that may sound.

Of course, the mother would not accept such a statement. The child was placed in a psychiatric ward, where she was described as having a grotesquely arched back, her arms and legs drawn up, her eyes staring blankly, and drooling through clenched teeth.

Her parents went to see her every day. Her mother would hold her, talk and sing to her, and take her outside in the sunshine. Then suddenly, four months later, a nurse noticed that the child was following her with her eyes and even smiled. Her parents took her home, first on weekends. Finally, a month later, because of her improvement, she left the hospital.

"The stimulation of having her family around and her sheer joy over being home caused her to progress steadily," said her mother. The physical therapists from the hospital came to her home. According to the last report, the child was being placed in a special school. She goes back and forth by bus. "She even has a glow she never had before," her mother added.

Having a child who is not normal is a terrible blow to parents. I felt it was my job to soften the blow, to help them accept it, to reinforce their strength, to help them understand, and to hold out hope. At first, some parents resented me, were even jealous if their child showed affection toward me. A foster parent once accused me of trying to "take over"; a grandmother once complained that I had "awakened" their grandchild and made the child more difficult. But I understood the frustration behind such complaints.

To be a foster parent of a disturbed child is difficult. Most of the foster children had been in several different homes and had adjusted to none. They came to us hungry for love; but if you gave them too much, they would collapse. This actually happened one time. I learned that one of the foster children was to have a birthday. I asked the doctor attending him if we could give him a little birthday party. The doctor at first advised against it and then yielded to our desire, saying, "I hope you aren't giving him too much." We gave him the party, and it was too much. He became so upset that he broke windows trying to get out. So I learned, too, in the process of helping these children.

We did have group sessions with the parents, and we found

they were helped by the discussions. Parental involvement is important. I was interested to learn that at the Judevine Center for autistic children in St. Louis (the nation's first center providing for the rehabilitation and education of autistic children) mothers—and fathers who can manage it—attend a three-week training program. Many mothers stay with their children every day and are a part of the therapy program. Deviant behavior is often encouraged by family attitudes. Lois Blackwell, head of the Judevine Center, believes that when a child is constantly out of control, someone is rewarding him for it. The typical pattern in most households is to let a child alone when he is "good" and give him attention when his behavior is "bad"—an attitude which reinforces autistic tendencies. "That is why we must train parents along with their children," Mrs. Blackwell says.

I have one more message for parents. We should ask ourselves the questions: Do we undignify our children? Do we order them about and, while they are trying to please us, forget to say "thank you"? If we do, we have taken away joy and replaced it with resentment.

When a parent screams at a child for something which simply annoys the parent, he should ask himself, "Would I be screaming at an adult who did or said the same thing?" Probably not. Such is the test that I would like more parents to apply when they speak to their children.

If we expect our children to live in a better world tomorrow, we have to give them dignity and respect and honesty to make them better citizens.

When I worked with student observers from Swarthmore College and with young parents whose children were attending the nursery day school, I used examples such as these to show them how easy it was to turn a difficult habit or behavioral problem into a constructive experience. The situations and solutions were ones I had experienced with children many times both as a parent and as a teacher.

1. *The Situation*

When a child refuses to eat an adequate meal, there is often a great deal of anxiety on the part of the parent. The child senses this and becomes anxious or more obstinate. Pretended indifference is a good policy. The child should be given the responsibility of eating, and eating should become a pleasurable experience. Frequently, parents put too much on a plate, thus discouraging the initial desire to eat. Here is one way I have suggested in which parents might handle the situation. I have tried it more than once; so I know it works.

Suzi's mother called her for supper. Suzi slowly walked into the room, sat down at the table, and said with her usual determination, "I don't want any supper. I'm not hungry."

This time her mother said, "Tonight I have a surprise for you. Here is your supper." She handed Suzi a plate, and on it there was one green pea!

"But that's only one little pea," she said, obviously puzzled.

Her mother smiled and said: "If you want another helping, just let me know, and I'll pass you the bowl." Suzi ate her one pea and asked for more.

"Would you like a spoonful of warm potatoes?" Her mother passed her the bowl. Suzi helped herself.

The Solution

In this case the mother helped the child to accomplish eating to her own capacity. Suzi was proud of herself for being able to ask for more. She also enjoyed the experience of serving herself.

2. *The Situation*

Children are sometimes curious, sometimes embarrassed, when they see a handicapped person. Parents find their frank questions hard to handle in a diplomatic way. Usually, their first impulse is to say "sh" to the child and apologize to the person who was the subject of the barrage of questions. Here is one way to handle the situation.

Mary's mother lifted her out of the car and handed her a pair of crutches. It was Mary's first day at nursery school. When Tommy and Peter saw her, they ran up and asked, "What are those?"

"Let me have them—please let me have a turn!"

"Can't you walk without them?"

Mary's teacher said, "Tommy, Mary is learning and those crutches are helping. Peter, will you show Mary how you are learning to swing on a rope."

The Solution

The concept of learning gave Mary a positive feeling of accomplishment and gave Tommy and Peter a satisfactory answer to their questions. This same solution can be used when children ask why someone has "funny eyes" or wears a hearing aid or rides in a wheelchair.

3. *The Situation*

It is, of course, impossible and inadvisable to confine a child within a fenced area at all times. Children need freedom, and they also need to know rules of safety at an early age. By appealing to the child's imagination, a mother can teach her preschooler the meaning of "out of bounds."

David backed his tricycle out of the garage and went for a long ride down the driveway and along the sidewalk. A few houses away, there was a doctor's office, where cars came in and out at frequent intervals. David's mother watched him as he approached the driveway and called out, "David, come back. You're *out of bounds.*"

David looked puzzled. And then his mother explained about the cars and said, "See these two trees on this side of the doctor's driveway? We will pretend they are gates, and we will remember to stay on this side of them. If we go through our pretend gates, we are *out of bounds*."

The Solution

David's mother was able to make a game of placing a boundary beyond which he was not permitted to ride. More important, David enjoyed the responsibility that his mother had placed within his capacity. She trusted him to stop at the "pretend" gates. Boundaries can be made with a clothesline on the ground, a small barrel or sawhorse at the end of a driveway, or a long stick—just to indicate the stopping point.

IV
Discipline or Despair

I sometimes think everything I have to say has probably been written a hundred times by now. My work with the clinic took place in the early 1960s, and there were few guidelines then. The Montessori movement which had been popular in the early 1900s was being reintroduced in America during this period. Controversial though it was, it spread rapidly and this time gained a permanent home in all parts of the country.

I remember reading that Maria Montessori, who was born in 1870 and was the first Italian woman to earn an M.D. degree, was an early specialist in the training of mentally defective children. Her emphasis was on the sensory experience in learning. She believed that education should be based not only on the great responsiveness of children's senses but also on their own desire to master real skills. The teacher, she believed, should let the child set his own pace. She would help them help themselves. Her method taught that a child who is bothering others or being destructive should be stopped or diverted but not scolded or punished. She was particularly concerned that children learn for themselves, and also that they not be squelched by disapproval.

I probably always identified with Maria Montessori's ideas, even before I was fully aware of them. I could feel very strongly the need for both approval and discipline in dealing with all children. The frustrated parents who brought their children to the clinic had long since given up on one or the other or both.

The parents or foster parents of emotionally disturbed children

who arrived at the clinic were sadly confused. When they sat down to relate the child's history they usually presented contradictory stories. They seemed only to be sure of one thing: their child was somehow "not right." The parents would come to the clinic feeling it was the last resort. They had, more than likely, tried to enter the child in a private nursery school or public school kindergarten, only to be rejected.

The parents of the more severely disturbed autistic children were at their wits' end. Often the child had been ruling the household, overactive, uncommunicative, often self-destructive, and always baffling. Would we take the child? Could we help?

In working with both the disturbed children and the autistic children—and we worked with them together in the clinic setting—we teachers discussed one common thing, that they seemed to have so little discipline at home. By discipline I do not mean locking a child in a room (as some parents did for hours and days on end) or whipping them or beating them. I am speaking of holding limits. A child knows whether he is in command of the home. He knows when his mother feels guilty and says to herself, "I'll let him have his way today, but tomorrow I'll really mean business." He not only feels guilty, but he loses respect for her.

One reason we liked to get the children at an early age was the feeling that we could more easily break a pattern of aggressive behavior—or plain dogged control—within the home. Temper tantrums begin, I have told many parents, when you do not demand of children the best that they can give, when you don't respect them and have expectations for them. Much of our dif-

ficulty in working with the children had to do with the fact that they had developed patterns of not hearing what they did not want to hear and not doing what they did not wish to do. It would take most of our physical strength and mental agility to guide the children into a path of behavior that would fit the rhythm of progressive growth.

Our method of defining limits of behavior was simple. When a child was disruptive, we would remove him from the activity for a short period of time, perhaps placing him on a mat or a chair to watch from the sidelines. Often another child would ask, "What's happened to Johnny?" Our answer would be, "Johnny is learning."

We would return the child to the activity before it was completed so that he could feel that he had had the opportunity to learn self-control. He would therefore finish the activity on a positive note.

As I have mentioned before, the doors were not locked at the clinic. The inside doors are swinging ones; so we could move about more easily. One autistic child was brought to us because he kept running away. Any open door at home or elsewhere was his escape hatch. We knew this when he joined our group. We knew we would have to help him learn not to run away before we could work with him in other ways.

The first few times he darted through the door, I caught him in time and placed him on the mat, saying each time, "When Kenny is big enough not to run away, then he will be big enough to come to the table again." One day I watched this nonverbal little boy walk over to a large picture—a painting of a cat—resting against the wall, and flip it down. When I put it up, he would knock it down. So I put the picture in a closet in the next room.

The next day, I decided to use the picture for a prop. I placed the picture against the swinging doors. He looked at it and flipped it down. But he did not dart out the door that day. The next day, I left the picture in the closet; and when he came, he looked for it, found it, brought it from the closet, and set it in front of the door. Then he looked at me and smiled. He had gotten the message. He never tried to run away again. He learned to control his quickness, and we would take him on walks with us, confident that he would not let us down.

Jimmy was another child who needed to know his limits. He was fond of the color yellow and would even carry the yellow page section of the telephone book to his mat during rest period. He became attached to a yellow plastic toy baseball bat. Of course, he knew I would never use it as a weapon, but it served me well as a way to discipline him. When he was roaming around the room, making far too much noise, I had only to pick up the little yellow bat and he knew that I meant for him to start a more constructive activity.

One day, when I was changing one of the younger children who was not yet toilet trained, Jimmy left the music group to see what I was doing. I asked him to return to his group, but he just stood there. I noticed the bat lying on the table nearby, and I said, "Jimmy, will you please hand me the yellow bat?" He handed it to me with a knowing look and returned to his group.

I would use food to communicate. If a child was crying or angry, I would peel an apple. Invariably, the child would stop and watch the long red cork-screw peel unwind from the apple, and that would be the end of the tantrum. One child would often arrive in the morning clutching two sharp pencils, one in each hand. We would relieve him of the pencils, giving him two large crayons to hold. Sometimes I would cut two pieces of fruit and let him hold them, and this seemed to bring noticeable relaxation and trust.

Some of the children finally learned to know their limits and would even teach each other. I remember a time when two of the children with whom I was preparing lunch kept doing something I considered potentially dangerous. I was letting them cut the celery for tuna salad, and the two were wielding table knives with abandon. I was ready to stop them but silently hoped they would control themselves so that I would not have to say "Don't."

Tommy, who was watching me while his companions continued to flirt with danger, finally said, "Come on, now, stop that. It makes Mimi's legs hurt!"

I can remember only once resorting to a spanking. Greg, a child I felt had great promise, arrived angry. He disliked his new shorts and his sneakers and showed it by screaming and jumping up and down. Finally I took him into my little office and said, "Mimi loves you dearly, Greg, but we must stop this noise. It isn't making you happy or anybody else. I believe I will have to spank you." I took him over my lap and patted his bottom very gently. He stopped crying and looked up at me, said, "Kiss, kiss," and kissed me on the cheek. Gregory wanted help. He wanted someone to care enough to be angry with him, to share his anger, and to help him control it. This is really what the normal child wants from the adult, too. He wants to be respected, but he wants to have controls.

I guess my approach toward discipline could be called "early behavior modification." I would reward appropriate behavior with a smile, a pat, a piece of fruit, an encouraging word. Inappropriate behavior never went unnoticed. As I described before, the child would in some way be taken from the group or activity in which he was engaged to know I expected more from him. All of this I did with affection, and the children began to show affection. The autistic ones even began to sing and to speak.

At the Judevine Center in St. Louis, teaching techniques have been developed that are far more refined than mine were. The teachers use a "magic light," regulated so that whenever the child sits in the chair the light is on; when he leaves his seat, the light goes off. The child is helped to realize that his behavior controls the light; if he wants breakfast, he must sit in the chair. He has to establish an eye-to-eye exchange with the teacher and sit still before being rewarded with food.

The children at the Judevine Center who do not conform to the class's behavior standards are put in a well-ventilated, well-lighted "timeout" room for three to five minutes. The room is within earshot of the class, and the child always reenters before the activity is finished.

I mention these developments because they are the "modern" version of the techniques which I began using three decades ago. Perhaps they are more effective than peeling an apple or having a child sit on his mat. But our goals are the same, and whatever works should be tried and tried again.

Another behavioral-oriented school, patterned after the Judevine Center, is the Developmental Learning Center of Wayne County, Detroit, Michigan. Again, it was the parents who promoted the new programs for their autistic children. At the Wayne County center the child's reward is his favorite food, along with a pat or a hug from his teacher and such approving words as "Good working" or "Good acting" or "Good looking at me." The words are as much a reward as the food.

At the David School in Chicago, an effective experiment with the use of hand language is going on. They have found that to give the autistic children a way to communicate with their hands has led to their ability to finally articulate words. Psychologist Margaret Creedon believes, as I do, that children learn from other children; and her schools encourage them to relate to each other. Emphasizing group experience and group approval, the David School has been critical of programs that rely solely on the one-to-one relationship between child and therapist. That has been my feeling from the beginning. If you want to have children relate to others, then relating is what you must have them do. "We don't want these kids talking for M&M's all their lives," is the way Ms. Creedon puts it! Children must realize that communication is its own reward. They are, in a sense, *learning* joy.

In Mary MacCracken's book *Lovey* (J. B. Lippincott Co., 1976), which concerns her experience as a teacher of disturbed children, I noted that she, too, believes that children push each other into maturation. "There is no better teacher than another child," she says.

Ms. MacCracken would have the children test each other out,

observing in a quiet way their ability to relate. She found, as I have so often:

> Children can't begin to learn until they feel safe, and they can't feel safe until they are honestly and completely accepted. A child like Hannah—hospitalized at six weeks, shut in closets, locked out of her home, beaten by both her brother and her father, rejected by the public school—not only feared other people, she feared herself as well. Hannah knew she was different; she knew that parts of her were frightening, both to herself and others. But she didn't know how to change. She couldn't cut herself in pieces, divide herself in two, bring in only the good part. She needed to know that she was welcome, all of her, the good and the bad.

V
Working with Children— Some Case Histories

Gary

Gary was one of my first charges, when the nursery unit of the Child Guidance Clinic began in 1963. I would like to discuss him here because he was a prime example of the extent to which we could help these children—and he demonstrated our limitations as well.

When he came to us, Gary was a severely withdrawn six-year-old. Later he would be diagnosed as brain-damaged, but we were not aware of this at the time. He was unable to converse with anyone. When he tried, which was rarely, his speech was badly garbled. The psychologist's tests placed Gary at a three-year verbal level, which seemed generous to me. His nonverbal tests demonstrated "normal" ability.

Gary was large for his age. He seemed nearly as tall as I. He walked on his toes, spit, and drooled. He banged his head at the slightest opportunity or whenever something or someone displeased him. He often refused to eat. When he did, he ate like a puppy, never holding a utensil. As a result of these unlovely characteristics, he had been all but discarded by his family. His parents had five other children, and of course Gary added more than his share to the confusion and clutter in that household.

When his mother brought him to us that first day, she remarked as she entered the nursery that Gary would enjoy the piano and would probably want to play it—but that we should not allow him to touch it.

"He will pick off the keys. So you must watch him all the time!" she warned. I suggested that he might like to have a damp cloth and wipe off the keys while he was there, but his mother insisted that he would be destructive. He never did fulfill her fears. But he did fulfill my expectations. He often went to the piano—and played it softly and well.

One month after Gary entered the nursery, I wrote in my report to the caseworker:

> Gary got out of the car all by himself and seemed anxious to come. He went to the piano and played nicely. . . . At the lunch table we had another hamburger because Chip had missed the picnic before vacation. Gary would take a piece and spit it on the floor; and each time, he cleaned it up himself. I said to him, "Look at me, Gary," and I took his chin in my hand very gently and repeated, "Look at me, please." He did this, and with a smile; so I said, "Any boy who can play a piano so gently and nicely, and who can put puzzles together so well, I am sure can eat and drink well also." Gary smiled, and after that he tried very hard.

July 15, 1963:

> Today flowers came for my birthday and Gary said, "flowers!" When I put on a smock for painting, I put my face against his, and he smiled and seemed to like it. I called him "lover" and you could almost hear him purr.

October 8, 1963:

> A very good music period. I put my hand on my throat and we sang. They all did the same. Gary seemed to like the idea, and I had him put his fingers on my throat while I sang. It seemed to help him open his mouth, and words came out as he put his fingers on his own throat. He comes to me when we start action in music. Then I step out of the picture and he goes on by himself. A very interesting morning.

October 29, 1963:

> Gary built a wonderful train bridge and slide. While he
> worked he kept saying, "Mimi say stop spitting, stop spit-
> ting, Gary." He changed his track three times, and when I
> asked him what else Mimi said to him, he smiled and said,
> "Mimi said, 'Gary, make a tunnel'!" and he did.

Some of Gary's fears and dislikes were beginning to drop away.
In the beginning, he had been afraid to move from one room into
another, but now he enjoyed walking down the long hall to the
bathroom. He loved to have me help him wash his hands in the
warm sudsy water. It was a form of communication between us.

Before going to the toilet, he would spit. I think the reason he
did this was because I would tell him when he spit on the floor,
"We do not spit on the floor. If we must spit, we spit into the
toilet!" Then I would hand him a tissue to wipe up the mess. He
finally stopped spitting except during an occasional trip to the
bathroom.

When we moved into the new Delaware Child Guidance Clinic
on the outskirts of Media, I was afraid Gary might find the
change difficult. But he met the situation according to my highest
hopes, with a great deal of appreciation and understanding of its
beauty and the way the light of the sun came in.

Early in 1964 Gary came up for reevaluation. I had watched
him grow in understanding, in appreciation, and in wisdom. But
when it came time for him to be tested by the psychologist, he
found it hard to pay attention or to control himself. For the first
time, he received a diagnosis. The EEG showed that he was suf-
fering from brain damage—which was the primary reason for his
garbled speech.

We worked harder after that to help him to express his needs.
On June 1, 1964, I wrote:

> Gary is growing and moving into a new pattern. He does
> not need to sit by me at the table. Thursday we served milk
> and potato chips. Gary held out until the end and then

asked me to move from the table in order that he might spill his milk! He finally drank it instead, and when he went out to meet his mother, she asked him what had made him so happy.

His relations with his brothers and sisters improved during this period. Often, when his mother came to pick him up at noon, I would walk out to the car carrying a little basket of pretzels or crackers— whatever was left over from our tea party. I would let him hold it and pass it to his twin sisters and other siblings. This gave him great joy, and there began a new feeling between Gary and his family, one which had never existed before.

On July 21, 1964, I wrote:

> It has been most interesting to watch him develop from a very tense, fearful little boy who seemed to understand all that was said to him, but was alone and unwanted in his home and in the outside world. . . . He learned to relate and feel the new limits and the guidance and love of an adult. The other children here love him, for he is a boy with a deep sense of joy and sorrow, and in all of his actions he has never hurt anybody but himself.
>
> He has learned to taste new foods and to drink milk, and to swallow with ease, which was not his pattern. [Until a few months earlier he had eaten only baby foods.] I feel that Gary is ready to move into a new experience of learning. He enjoys his family and knows that they love him and are proud of his new achievements. He trusts the adults and has learned that he has much to give as well as to receive.

After he had spent the summer day camp with us, we decided to put him in a special class in the county public schools. Gary's behavior was not acceptable there, and after two months he was brought back to our group. We put him into the afternoon unit with children who knew how to play and express themselves. His speech continued to improve.

I learned a great deal from this experience with Gary. He progressed—*blossomed* I think is the better word—and there was no longer any thought that he might have to be placed in an institution. After he left the clinic, he was taught by tutor at home. We worked together for a while toward the goal of having him enter a special education unit in a regular school.

His home still leaves something to be desired, to be sure. There are now seven children and much confusion. This is not a restful atmosphere for Gary. He even complained about it to me. So at least he has learned to externalize a problem.

Rob

When six-year-old Rob was referred to the clinic, his report indicated there was little wrong with him except that he found it hard to relax and kept his family awake most of the night. In a day or two, we learned that he had no knack for playing with other children and was not interested in food, in eating—all he wanted to do, in fact, was sit in his chair, rocking, and watch television.

He formed attachments to inanimate objects, as so many of these children do. In his case it was a record player, a pipe, a doorknob. He would be perfectly oblivious to any human being near him in the room or at the table, however. And his walk indicated that he did not think of himself as a real person; he slouched along as though he had no red blood in him, no pride in himself. And yet he seemed sophisticated, an unusual trait and an unpleasant one in a six-year-old, especially combined as it was with a kind of conceit.

Rob was always clean and beautifully dressed. His hands were carried like club feet, with the thumbs apparently immovable. He never used these thumbs, never separated them from his hands to pick up a cup or a block or box.

This was the first thing I noticed about him, and so I began to talk with him about his hands. They were lifeless and limp, as I discovered when I picked them up and held them in mine. Children of this type enjoy having you hold their hands in your own or wash them. They enjoy this intimacy. I began by teaching Rob to shake hands with firmness and feeling. While he was performing this act, I would say, "Ah—but you have such wonderful hands! And your thumbs are so important!" Then, while we took a walk, I would say, "Let's step as though we were proud of ourselves—we're *real*." He soon picked up the hints and began acting on them.

His smile was like that characteristic of the disturbed—it was "only from the neck up," so to speak. It was not a warm smile, and his giggle was light and rather silly. His speech, which was pitched high, had no depth to it. This became especially evident when an adult entered the room. Then he would immediately stop whatever he was doing and run to the adult, talking very fast in this high-pitched voice.

I began to talk to him about what was expected of him now that he was six years old. We went over and over the fact that when an adult entered a room it was not any of his business, and he need not stop what he was doing and try to attract the adult's attention.

While I was working with him this way, I came to find out that he had been dominating his entire household by the simple process of refusing to go to bed and to sleep at night. Often it would be nearly 2 a.m. before he could be prevailed upon to lie down. He had also developed the unnerving habit of asking his mother every single morning what she had planned for dinner that night. If it turned out to be something he disliked, he would be angry and unhappy all day long.

In most cases, these children are very poor eaters and only want to eat certain things. They do not try new things. So at lunch period one day I began to discuss with him why he was so interested in what his mother was having for dinner and why he was so unhappy if it was not exactly what he wanted. This discussion made him very sullen and angry. He refused to answer me.

So I said to him, "You are a six-year-old boy. Only a six-year-old boy. We want you to be happy, like any other six-year-old.

Your mother is in charge of the household, and she has wonderful ideas about cooking, just as your father, who is a doctor, is wonderful at fixing up people. You are a small boy. You can't fix up people and you can't cook the way your mother does. Your job is to be yourself and to let your mother and your father be themselves. You let your mother work with the cooking, and you work here at being a six-year-old with Mimi!"

After a number of these conversations, he began to understand that he was expected to accept his mother's decisions about food and to try new foods when they were offered at home, a thing he had begun to do at school. He also began to be aware that he need not feel that he was in personal command of everything that went on. He learned that he was only a small boy with a small part to play, even though this was a very important part in the clinic. As soon as we could, we made him accept the responsibility of seeing himself in the total picture, as a part of a whole world of different beings. Then he began to walk with his head up, his voice was pitched lower, and his smile gained some depth. He became so busy with his own work and play that when an adult came into the room he did not feel he had to reassure himself that he liked this adult or was not afraid of this adult. He kept right on with his own work.

We expected more of him at school; and during the two years we worked with him, not only he underwent a real change, but his parents began to undergo a change as well. They had come in seeming like empty shells. Then they began to warm up a little. Their voices, too, began to have more depth.

Sometimes I cannot help feeling that some parents who brought their children to me at the clinics had not matured very much themselves. They seemed to have no clear image of themselves to transmit to their children, but at some point they would become used to the atmosphere, which was warm and helpful and friendly. When they became involved with the people who were dedicated to helping them and their children, they finally began to trust themselves as parents.

Nan

Soon after I started working with autistic children at the clinic, Dr. Dudley called me into his office. He was holding in his lap a little girl with beautiful features and long tangled blonde hair. She would not look at either of us. She seemed totally oblivious to all that surrounded her. She was so slight and frail and her skin was so sallow that I felt she must be undernourished.

Dr. Dudley explained that she was to enter the clinic day nursery (she was, as I recall, almost five years old). We talked with the parents at that session. Her father and mother were both busy

professionals. This was the second marriage for both, and Nan
was the only child of their marriage (although they also had a
bright older son who was a child of her first marriage). Nan, they
said, had never spoken a word. They had taken her to
pediatricians and other specialists trying to find the source of her
problem. She would hum incessantly and leap about like a
frightened fawn. They brought her to the clinic, anxious to
cooperate, but amazingly naive about their role in Nan's development—or lack of it.

We had started the technique of having the parents work with
the psychiatrist who was helping the child. In addition to my role
as Nan's teacher, there was a caseworker who followed her
progress; we all worked as a team. I truly wondered at first if we
could help Nan. Her pattern of behavior seemed so set. She would
leap about, making noises, but saying no words and never in-
dicating that she understood ours. Yet something about her made
us all want to help her find herself. Her parents' home, when I
visited it, reflected the taste of a career-oriented mother. The fur-
niture and decor were modern and cold. Nan climbed on the
fireplace mantle when we entered the livingroom, much to my
astonishment. As I recall, no one in the family expressed surprise
or even seemed to notice. I realized then why she expected to have
so much freedom in the clinic and why we would have to harness
it with patient firmness. The garden of their home was lovely, but
I was shocked to see that her father, who loved Nan dearly and
wanted to help her so desperately, had purchased for her en-
tertainment in the backyard a suspended steel wire with a handle
on a pulley that would permit the child to "sail" across the yard
on a sort of monorail! That was certainly the last thing Nan
needed, since she was inclined to jump and climb and "sail"
through the air *most* of the time.

Nan seemed to love music. So with Adeline's help—and, of
course, the help of the clinic team—we somehow got through to
her. She would at first only respond to music. She loved to watch
Adeline at the piano, and her first words came forth in a song the
children were singing. One of our young volunteer assistants had

asked Nan's mother if she would let her take Nan to *The Sound of Music* at a nearby theater. Her mother consented, and the music in the show kept Nan spellbound. After that, Nan began to participate in group singing.

We had Nan in our clinic group for five years. She became one of our most talented young artists. In fact, she could do almost anything with her hands. As she progressed, she began to look healthier. I concerned myself at one point with her tangled hair and showed her, holding a mirror, how much better it looked when we brushed and combed it. I even washed it several times and combed it out. She began to appreciate herself. And when this happened, she began to notice others. One day she touched my head and said, "Your hair is silver." That was a lovely reward for our efforts.

Nan's mother drove with such speed that we all feared she would throw herself and her child through the windshield when she came to a screeching stop each morning to drop her off. Near the end of Nan's time with us, her mother did have an accident in town, and Nan was able to leave the car and get help for her mother. She had come a long way.

As Nan progressed, her mother became a more gentle and less harried person. She told us her son had benefitted, too, from our helping Nan and that the family was no longer fearful for Nan's future. Nan went from the clinic to a very fine private school for special children, which will take her through high school.

Headstart—Another Dimension

I consider the summer of 1965 the time I completed my training as a teacher. With ten years of nursery school teaching of normal children followed by three years of work with severely disturbed children, I found myself in the midst of a summer Headstart session for so-called deprived children. I learned a lot and so did they.

Let me begin by saying that the term *deprived children* should never have been used with this program, because it is so negative. I would rather think of them as *valuable children,* children with potential. We watched some of them become transformed from timid, anxious children to aggressive and even hostile children and finally to children who were relaxed and comfortable in our nursery unit. In five weeks I felt they had begun to be aware that they had a place in a world that was not hostile and that fighting and fear did not have to be a part of the pattern.

The fifteen to twenty children in the first Headstart program in Delaware County came to us at noon each day for eight weeks. We were running a summer camp program for fifteen of our disturbed children during the morning, so this was a full day. We could not have done it without the help of a college graduate aide, three student volunteers, and a sixteen-year-old boy who

became our cook and learned to feed twenty people a hot dinner at noon in addition to carrying on all our other activities.

The students working with us learned more than they ever will from books, and I feel sure they will be better parents for the experience. One example stands out in retrospect. One of our students spoke in a rather abrupt manner to the children. She would say things like "Do this" and "Do that" and "Go here," "Go there" or "Take your elbows off the table." I had known her most of her life and felt sure she sensed my disapproval; so I talked with her about it. We discussed the art of conversation during mealtime. She protested, "But, Mimi, I thought I was here to make them mind." I said, "No, we're here to live together. You don't talk down to them, you don't put your hand on top and push them down, but you reach down and bring them up to you. You want them to think of you as a friend."

I pointed out to her that she was good at tennis and the children would probably enjoy hearing about her sports activities. I was pleased the next day when I heard her asking the children questions that interested them and then telling them about her swimming and tennis achievements. The conversation rose, and on the days that followed, several children asked to sit at her table. Her own pleasure in this experience was great.

When the parents came to watch their children sing and dance and do their handicraft work (the temperature was ninety degrees, but no one complained), I felt we had reached these special people and they had accepted our help graciously. Often a Headstart volunteer would visit and ask us, "How do you think these children will act when they go back to their homes after such an exciting and varied experience?" Of course, they are not different from many of the foster children and underprivileged children I have had in the past at the clinic. And with them I have found that the enrichment and relationship have not made them unhappy with their home situation but rather more observant and more understanding of the things around them. So when the Headstart person asked me such a question, I would say, "It is like taking these children into a meadow. We find a daisy or a Queen Anne's Lace blossom, and we show it to them, and we enjoy it together. We give things to them with respect and share the joy that we have learned."

I think this is what we have handed to our Headstart children. We have made them more aware, and in the graciousness of sharing there is no feeling of sending them home to be unhappy and discontented. I rode home with them sometimes to see where and how they lived, and it was often very sad. But the conversations of these boys and girls in the car as we approached their homes showed me that they were happy and joyful and without self-pity or false pride. It was a good lesson for us all.

George

The story of George, told by his mother, illustrates better than I could tell how a positive approach can help parents help their own child. This account came to us in the form of a letter because she had heard we were writing this book.

I met Mimi when George was enrolled in Swarthmore Presbyterian Nursery School—at that point [1973] George was four and we felt there was something wrong, but various doctors had only come up with immaturity, maturational lag, and "let's wait and see." Mimi saw George once or twice a week when she would have a few children come to her clay table. Mimi's involvement with George was very small, but her involvement with me was monumental. In my eyes she gave me the "start" needed to face a difficult situation, and I've been able to build on that ever since.

It's really hard to put on paper what my husband and I felt at this point in our lives. Early in 1974 one doctor and his psychologist recommended that George go to a child psychiatrist—and that perhaps a bit of "shifting the mold" would make life easier for him. They still considered George a puzzle and felt that perhaps this might be the answer.

After seeing this doctor for six weeks, I casually asked if he had any idea of why George was having so much difficulty functioning. He said that George had a very serious problem, needed a great deal of help, and would always be different. It's interesting to me that as I think back those are the words I remember the most—"will always be different." I immediately asked what is wrong with being different—the doctor explained the type of "different" he meant. When I pressed for more familiar language, he said George fell into the category of *autism*. This all happened in ten minutes on our way out of the office.

What I really want to tell you about is how Mimi stood by—as only Mimi can do—and what she has done for me and in turn George.

After the doctor's diagnosis, my husband and I made an appointment to talk and get as much information as we could. George is our only child—a much loved and wanted little boy—and, I must say, a very dear person. I think probably we were handling all of this as well as anyone could. We had George see the doctor twice a week, which was costly for us, but at that point I probably would have sent him five times a week if we could have afforded it—and if my husband hadn't possessed a great deal of good judgment as well as love.

I don't remember what made me call Mimi, but I found myself at her house, sitting in the rocking chair, unfolding the story and what the future was supposed to hold. Before I had finished, but after I had related the conversation that "George would always be different," Mimi said, "Mary, I just want to tell you one thing—I'm not worried about George." I have tears right now as I think back to that. I think maybe an angel was speaking. That was the most blessed statement that has ever been said to me—and I know it was all I needed to hear.

I've often thought about how Mimi suddenly took George's problem and delivered it from the impossible and put it into reality as something we most certainly could deal with. I can't say for sure that the doctor wouldn't agree that the problem could be handled. I can only say that after listening to him, we had a very pessimistic outlook—full of the unknown, years of costly treatment, and heartbreak.

And today I can tell you we do have unknowns that we consider in a positive light. We do have expenses that we consider a part of our life and wouldn't think of depriving George of help. We do have frustrations, but they are merely part of our hard work, and after every frustration there seems to be growth and reward. We think George's future is positive, and we intend to provide the right environment so that he has every chance to make this positive growth.

That first day at Mimi's house was the beginning of many. I often found myself driving there after I dropped George off at school. To say that Mimi gave me loads of information or advice would be untrue—what Mimi did was listen. Mimi never said the doctor was wrong (at this point anyway) or that I should do anything differently with George—what Mimi did was to cause me to believe in myself. She kept saying, "What you give away you keep." Suddenly, instead of a bleak and negative future, I was beginning to take a day at a time—beginning to use the common sense that I had. Mimi never said, "Stop worrying." She merely would tell me wonderful stories from her childhood—stories from which I was able to gain something. At times I saw how a particular idea might work with George. Mimi had a wonderful way of pointing out George's strong points—such as his sensitivity, his lovely eyes, and his loving nature. It wasn't long before I was back on the track of a positive approach.

I've often thought about why I found such comfort and trust in Mimi, and I don't think it was just the fact that her thoughts about George were of a positive nature. My own parents gave us a great deal of comfort and support, but it was because of Mimi that I was able to accept the problem and move ahead. Mimi offers a strength that I haven't found in anyone else—it's *Mimi's gift*, like having a talent for art or music. Mimi has this wonderful gift of seeing and feeling that no amount of education could ever provide. I really knew nothing of Mimi's history or personal life when I first went to her with our problem—I just somehow knew that with the amount of time she had seen George she would know if the future was as bad as we had been led to believe.

As I came to know Mimi, she would relate stories to me of children she had known. I always loved the way she could laugh at so many situations that had to be so tense and frustrating, and now I've found that I can laugh at situations that seemed impossible at the time.

There must have been moments in our talks when she wanted to give me advice. There came a time when we had to make a decision on whether to continue with the doctor. Mimi knew how we wrestled with this. My innermost feelings said he had served his purpose; yet it was difficult to take away the professional who said he was the one qualified person to help our son. It was a big decision, but we made it. Only after we had left the doctor did Mimi say she thought we had made the right decision.

I guess it's no wonder that in frustrating periods with George I'd find myself sitting in Mimi's rocking chair. She never gave me a verbal answer to any problem, but somehow I'd leave knowing it would all work out. I wonder if this might have been what so many of the children felt when they were with Mimi. She gave them confidence felt strength from her wonderful insight, but she always knew when to step back and let them find it themselves.

As you can see Mimi has given me much. Hers is a friendship that I treasure. Hopefully I can give away some of what Mimi has given me.

George is doing well now and there is no doubt in our minds that he will make it. We are not without frustration, but with hope and a positive approach, frustration is no problem. George works hard, but he knows the support and love that his father and I feel for him—that's bound to count for a lot. He is seven now and goes to a special private school—a school for bright children who are not achieving; at the end of this year he got the class award for "the most all-around progress." The unknown can be so scary—or the unknown can be challenging and positive. I'm thankful I was guided to Mimi and so grateful for the guidance she was able to give me.

We don't know at this point if George will need to remain in a private school or if he'll be able to make it in a regular public school. It's hard to say with George. We still feel that growth is much in his favor.

Mary R.
July 1976

In 1974, I felt I had come full circle, from my early days at the Swarthmore Nursery School, the Delaware Child Guidance Clinic, then the Headstart program, and back to Swarthmore. But again, although I was determined to retire, I found that the hours seemed too empty. So I quietly made a place for myself as a "teacher-at-large" for a few hours each day at the Swarthmore Presbyterian Nursery School. I would bake the toast squares that the children loved to smell toasting and loved to eat as they waited for their parents to pick them up. I would just be around for the teachers to come to me with questions and for parents to discuss their problems or relate the progress of their children. I would handle the clay table and help the children in a childlike fashion—playing with them on their own level—to create something with their hands.

When I finally decided even that was too much because my husband, Pem, was homebound and needed my nursing care, I could rejoice in the fact that one of my daughters, Jody, her own children now grown, had taken a place there as a full-time teacher and assistant director.

And, of course, I still have my rocking chairs on the front porch, where I can talk with parents like George's mother.

VI

A Sense of Joy

Children have dignity. They like to know you are speaking specifically to them. As a teacher, whenever I addressed a child, I would always call him by name to help build his self-image. Over the years there have been so many children passing through the nursery school, the clinic, and my own front door that I could not possibly remember every name of every child every time I saw him. So I call them all "Sweeter." It is a name that reflects my love and admiration for them, and they respond to it as one does when an endearing nickname is used.

I have always spoken to children in a voice that would please them, even when I was being firm. I would repeat such phrases as "Mimi is proud of you" or "you're learning" or simply "Mimi loves you." And sometimes they would come back to me: "Aren't you proud of me, Mimi?" or "See, I'm learning!"

Sometimes I would find a special word or phrase and we would all talk about it. For example, we would discuss what it was to have "a sense of honor." It was a phrase they would take hold of and finally understand so that it became a part of their rhythm. They began to understand that "a sense of honor" meant for them to learn to use their own judgment, to take responsibility for their behavior. I'm sure they did not know the full meaning of the phrase, but they had a feeling for it and might ask, "Mimi, do I have a sense of honor?" or "Am I using my sense of honor?"

You could see in their eyes that they were thinking about achieving a new goal. I might answer them by saying that "to have a sense of honor, you must love yourself," or "when you learn to let someone else go first, you will have a sense of honor."

I used these phrases with my normal children in the Swarthmore nursery school long before I become involved with the more seriously disturbed at the Child Guidance Clinic. They needed to know what I expected of them. They needed to be treated with dignity. I would help them find a sense of joy. I would try to help them achieve a goal and build confidence in themselves. When I think about letting children grow to their full capacity, I remember a little four-year-old boy whose parents had built a home on a lot behind our house, so that we got to know each other very well indeed. He attended the nursery school at the Swarthmore Presbyterian Church. My bright-eyed little neighbor refused to participate. He just stood around, watching the others work and play. Several times during this period, I would return home to find that my door key, which I left in the mailbox, had been removed. I would look around for a bit, and then walk to the backyard. Each time, I would find the key by the gate which led to his house.

He had conscientious parents, very protective. They had built a fence around their house—a thing I do not condone. A child should learn his own limits; to be hemmed in takes away his self-respect and his ability to gain confidence in himself. I have often found that a child who has been fenced in or confined to a playpen is more inclined to wander away when he is finally released. The child who plays in open space will make his own boundaries after having had them given to him by a loving parent.

When I found the key by the little gate, I knew the child was asking for help in some direction. A talk with his mother brought out the fact that he had reverted to bed-wetting and had begun to treat his little sister unkindly. So I began to watch at nursery school to see what he had not yet accomplished. There are certain things a four-year-old should be doing to complete his image of himself. I took him to a tricycle and found that he refused to get on it. He said he "couldn't." For the next few days, he and I spent twenty minutes to half an hour going back and forth on that tricycle until he had mastered it. He then became proud of himself, and took to doing many others things he had avoided before, such as playing on the swings, slide and the jumping board.

One day I suggested that he bring his tricycle through the gate to our driveway, because there was no sidewalk in front of their house. I took a clothesline prop, and he and I laid it across the drive, to show him where the cars would come and where he must stop.

Soon my key stopped disappearing from my mailbox. He stopped wetting his bed. He had clearly reached a new plateau.

Another example of letting a child grow occurred when we were working with a four-year-old in the clinic. He would not speak at all and would avoid eye-to-eye contact, which is typical of the autistic children. He would often stand by the window, looking out; so I was sure the period of outdoor play meant a lot to him.

He understood everything we said perfectly. I watched him progress from the time when he was taking food away from others at the table and getting up and down constantly to the time, three months later, when he would sit with us, eat, and even seem to enjoy it.

One day, when it was snowing so hard that we decided we had better not venture out, he took my hand and pulled me toward the door. I said, "I'm sorry, Donny, but we can't go out today. We'll have to wait until a warmer day." He then went to get my assistant's hand and he pulled her to the door. When she gave him the same answer, he tried the two college students who were helping us. Their refusal brought anger, and he pushed chairs over.

The next day was sunny. As we were getting ready to go out, I put his coat down low so that he could reach it. I felt he was asking us to let him do more things. He left it there, and I finally said to him, "Will you please bring Mimi your coat, Donny." He walked away, pretending to ignore me. I went on outside, leaving him with Adeline, but he would not bring her the coat either. We placed him on a mat to think about what had happened, and he broke down and cried. Still he would not get his coat.

The following day was stormy again, and we couldn't go out. But we noticed Donny did not try to force us to take him out. And on the third day, when we prepared to go out, he brought me his coat without prompting. He was noticeably happier.

Often when I worked with a child consistently for three days, repeating the same pattern, he would pick it up on the fourth day. That was exciting.

Bob was another student who learned joy and acceptance in the day school. He had been diagnosed as hyperactive; and because of his size and aggression, he frightened the other children and even, occasionally, one of our young teachers. He would always race ahead to be the leader, pushing all others aside. So I decided to spend more time working with him. I would sit with him until he relaxed during some activity. One day, when the children were getting ready to come into the room for a snack around the table, I put my arms over the door to form a bridge. I noticed that Bob, for the first time, did not push ahead. When he reached my bridge, he said, "Mimi, I'm proud of you."

As we sat at the table, I repeated his statement to the children, and I added, "Do you know what Bob was really saying? He was saying that he was proud of *himself*." And so he had reached another plateau, and he was rewarded. Because he had learned more self-control, the children began to play with him. He went on from the clinic to a special private school in the area and later to a public high school, where the last I heard, he was doing well and had been selected as a safety guard.

Here, then, was the *sense of joy* we could help the children attain. We would give the child the background, the understanding, the patience, and the tremendous satisfaction with himself which comes about when he is able to accomplish the task which

has been set. We respected him, believed in his ability to do the task, and then we watched him catch this sense of joy in carrying out the job. This accomplishment would be a permanent part of his personality pattern.

Timmy was typical of the kind of children we had at the Child Guidance Clinic. He was a foster child who had been moved from home to home in his few short years; he had been in five "homes" in three years. These little people carry many, many sorrows in their hearts. It is always amazing to me, the fortitude they manage to build to protect them from agony. Their anger and resentment manifests itself in an inability to communicate—this is what brings them to the verge of being diagnosed autistic.

Timmy came to us with a very low I.Q. In a short time of working with Adeline and me, his I.Q. had gone up thirty points. It was a joyous experience to watch his whole attitude and expression undergo changes.

Sometimes it seemed like a miracle, even after watching the children a number of years. One Valentine's Day, in the clinic, somebody gave us some candy. On the top of the box was an empty little china heart-shaped box to be used, I suppose, on a bureau, to hold small objects or just to be decorative.

After we had eaten the mints from the box, the boys wanted to see what was in the little china heart. I opened it, and Timmy cried, "Oh—but, Mimi, there's nothing in it!"

And I said, "Yes, there is, Timmy. You put your finger in it and you can feel it."

We passed the heart around the table. There were seven little boys with me that day, and each one put his finger in it and passed it along. When it got back to Timmy, he put his finger in it, looked at his companions, and then at me and said, "Why, Mimi, it's full of love, isn't it?"

Timmy is now in regular school, holding to the pattern of rhythm set during those days. It was so simple, you see. We gave Timmy a trust in people, a trust in himself, and a sense of joy. He will keep this with him throughout his life because he came at an age when he was ready for something—some change which would bring meaning and clarity to his life.

The point is that these children know and feel within themselves when they are accomplishing something. You don't have to compliment them effusively either when they do step ahead. To compliment them when they do something that is within their own capacity would insult their self-confidence and their ability to grow. With dignity, we should let them keep this accomplishment for themselves. A ready smile or a twinkle of understanding in our eyes is enough.

I do not pretend to have created a new teaching method, but I hope that I have recorded some truths that will help parents and ultimately help their children.

Reaching back in time, where we can all find the beginning of teaching, I found this quotation from Socrates:

> Agree with me if I seem to speak the truth, or if not, withstand me might and main, that I may not deceive you as well as myself in my desire and, like the bee, leave my sting in you before I die. And now let us proceed.

To give children a sense of joy should be the goal of parents and teachers alike. It is not easy. But the time to begin is, for parents, when they are born, and, for teachers, the first day they venture

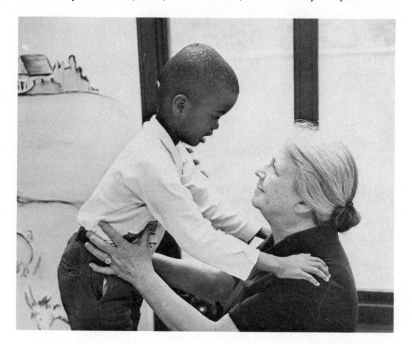

into the world of "other people" at nursery school and kindergarten. Both parents and teachers can become friends, warm and supportive, or persons who create the problems children have in later life—by repressing creativity, ignoring needs, and finding little pleasure helping the children to learn.

Teaching joy is easier to discuss than to achieve. It requires work, patience, forbearance, and understanding. But the reward of bringing joy to others is great. It is hard for us all to understand a paradox. We want to teach children to learn joy for their own sakes, not for ours. We want to hold them only long enough for them to find themselves. It has helped me to always remember that "what you give away, you keep—what you keep, you lose."

The photographs in this book have been provided by Henry L. McCorkle, the Philadelphia Evening Bulletin, *the Child Guidance and Mental Health Clinics of Delaware County, and* Presbyterian Life.